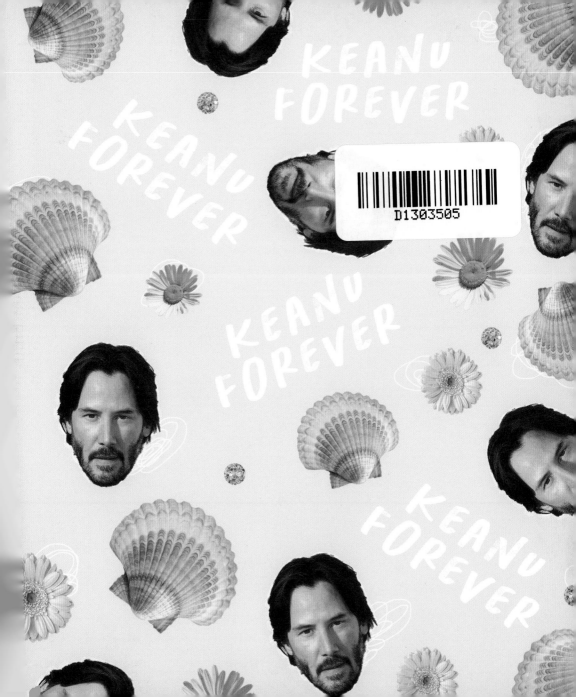

KEANU FOREVER

KEANU FOREVER

KEANU FOREVER

KEANU FOREVER

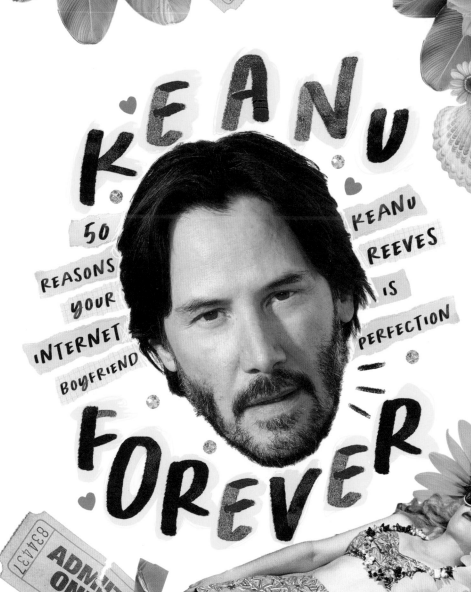

KEANU

50 REASONS YOUR INTERNET BOYFRIEND

KEANU REEVES IS PERFECTION

FOREVER

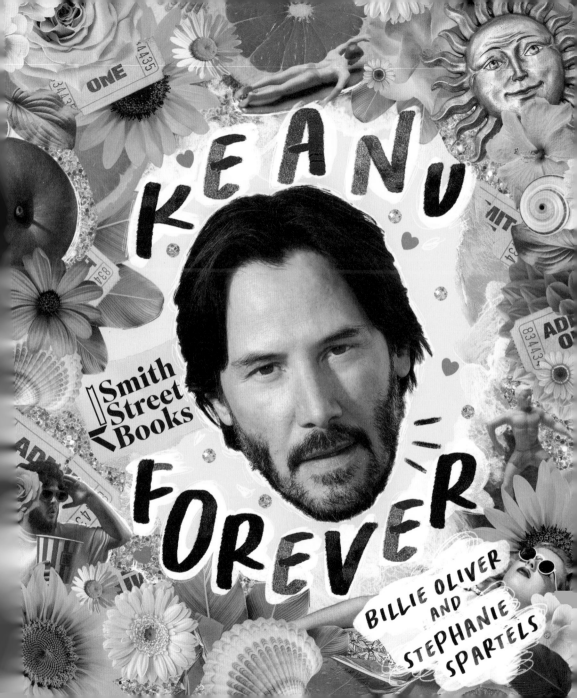

KEANU FOREVER

Smith Street Books

BILLIE OLIVER AND STEPHANIE SPARTELS

KEANU HAS BEEN ENTERTAINING US FOR OVER 35 YEARS —

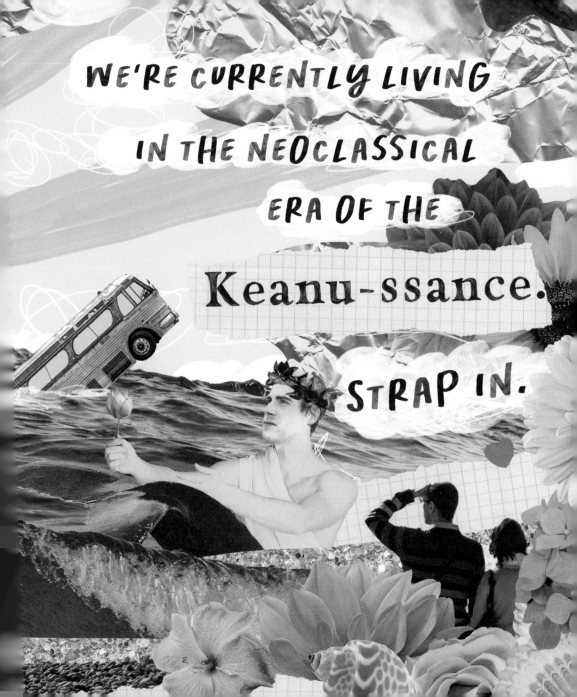

HE'S BEAUTIFUL IN AN OTHERWORLDLY SENSE. PERHAPS IT'S THE COMBINATION OF British, Portuguese, Native Hawaiian AND Chinese HERITAGE—

BUT THERE IS NO ONE ON EARTH WHO LOOKS QUITE LIKE KEANU.

THOSE FREQUENTLY FLOWING raven tresses ...

THAT INTENSE, CONTEMPLATIVE

THE SALT- AND -PEPPER FACIAL HAIR

THE FACT THAT HE SPEAKS FRENCH FLUENTLY.

THAT HIS NAME MEANS

'COOL BREEZE

OVER THE MOUNTAINS'

IN HAWAIIAN.

SIGH

HE'S A TRUE FAMILY MAN —

HE BOUGHT HIS MOM A HOUSE.

AND HIS BEST FRIEND IS HIS YOUNGER SISTER.

HE ALMOST BECAME A PROFESSIONAL ICE HOCKEY PLAYER, BUT WAS INSTEAD DRAWN TO ACTING AT AGE 15 (THANK THE GODS!).

HE'S A CITIZEN OF THE WORLD; BORN IN Beirut,

HOL

WOOD

HE GREW UP IN Sydney, Manhattan AND Toronto BEFORE MOVING TO Los Angeles.

HE LOVES TO HORSEBACK RIDE IN HIS SPARE TIME.

AND HAS PLAYED GUITAR IN THE BANDS DOGSTAR AND BECKY.

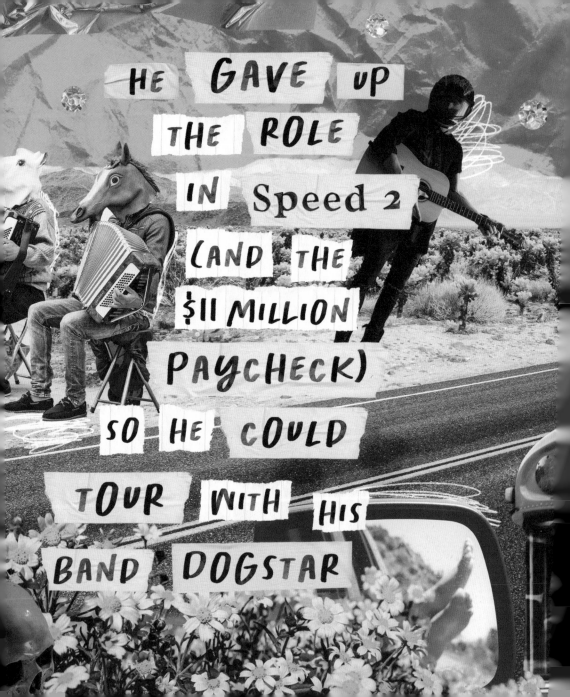

HE GAVE UP THE ROLE IN Speed 2 (AND THE $11 MILLION PAYCHECK) SO HE COULD TOUR WITH HIS BAND DOGSTAR

AND PLAY Hamlet ON STAGE.

HE HAS TWICE TAKEN LARGE PAY CUTS

SO THAT HE COULD SHARE THE SCREEN WITH LEGENDS GENE HACKMAN AND AL PACINO.

HE'S PLAYED THREE OF THE MOST ICONIC (AND BEST NAMED) CHARACTERS IN THE ACTION GENRE: Johnny Utah, Neo AND John Wick.

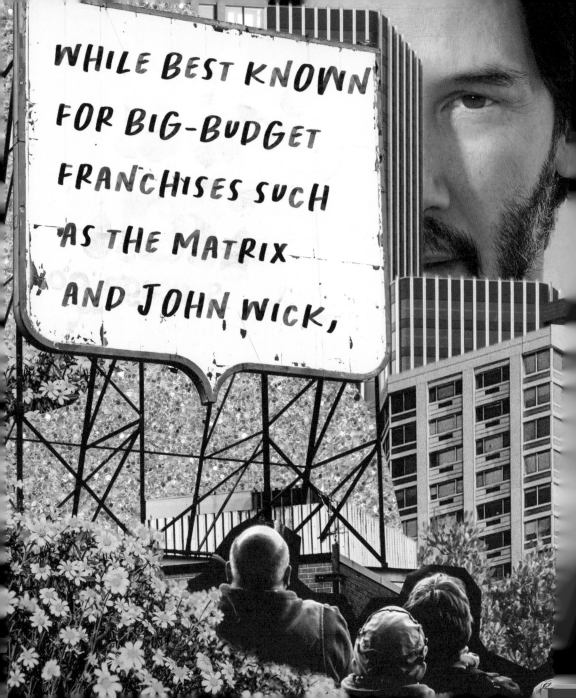

WHILE BEST KNOWN FOR BIG-BUDGET FRANCHISES SUCH AS THE MATRIX AND JOHN WICK,

HE'S ALSO PROLIFIC IN SMALL-BUDGET INDIE FILMS.

HE'S GENEROUS —
HE GAVE EACH OF
HIS STUNTMAN
ON THE MATRIX

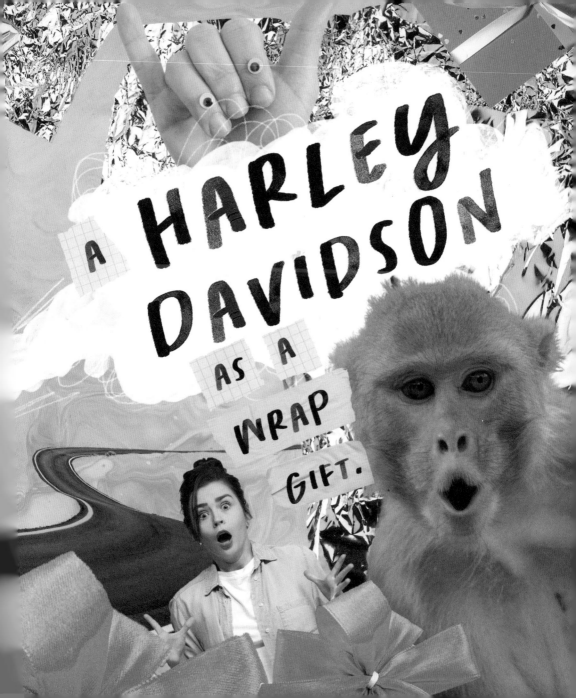

A HARLEY DAVIDSON AS A WRAP GIFT.

FOLLOWING THE SUCCESS OF THE FILM, HE GAVE MORE THAN HALF HIS BACK EARNINGS

FROM THE MATRIX TO THE SFX AND COSTUME DEPARTMENTS.

HE TURNED **55** LAST YEAR.

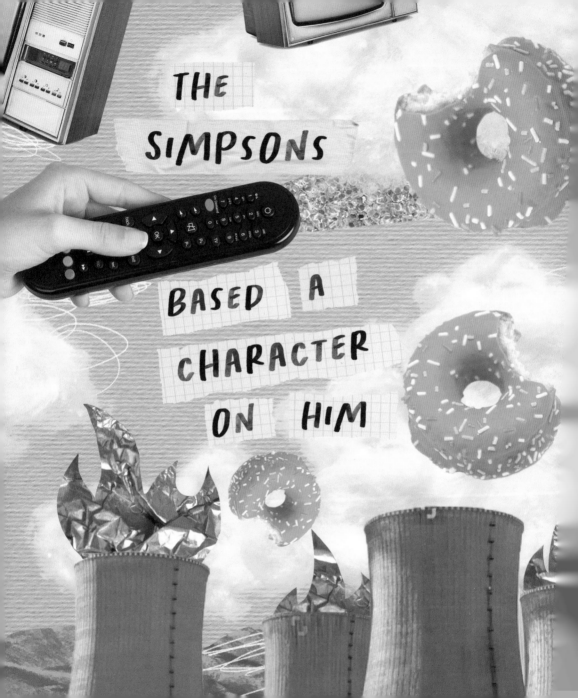

THE SIMPSONS

BASED A CHARACTER ON HIM

(NO,
IT
ISN'T
RALPH).

HE'S NOT AFRAID TO MAKE FUN OF HIMSELF

WITH SELF-REFERENTIAL APPEARANCES IN THE FILMS Keanu AND Always be My Maybe.

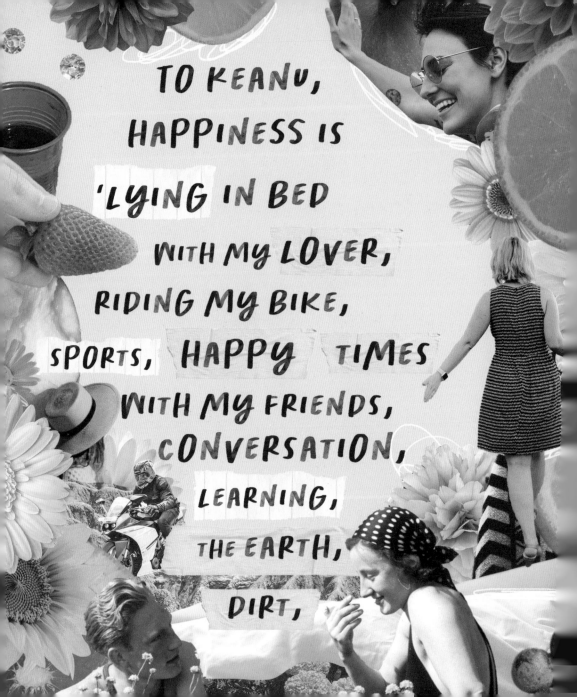

TO KEANU, HAPPINESS IS 'LYING IN BED WITH MY LOVER, RIDING MY BIKE, SPORTS, HAPPY TIMES WITH MY FRIENDS, CONVERSATION, LEARNING, THE EARTH, DIRT,

A BEAUTIFUL REPAST WITH FRIENDS, FAMILY WITH WINE AND GLORIOUS FOOD AND HAPPY TIDINGS AND ENERGY AND ZEST AND LUST FOR LIFE'

AFTER NEARLY
TWO DECADES OF
APPARENT SOLITUDE,
KEANU RECENTLY
STEPPED OUT
PUBLICLY
WITH HIS
AGE-APPROPRIATE
PARTNER,

ALEXANDRA

GRANT.

WE ALL
SWOONED,
HARD.

HE'S EXTREMELY DEDICATED,

LEARNING OVER 200 MARTIAL ARTS MOVES FOR THE John Wick MOVIES.

KEANU'S CREATIVE PURSUITS ARE MANY AND VARIED: FROM ACTING IN FILMS, ON STAGE AND IN VIDEO GAMES!

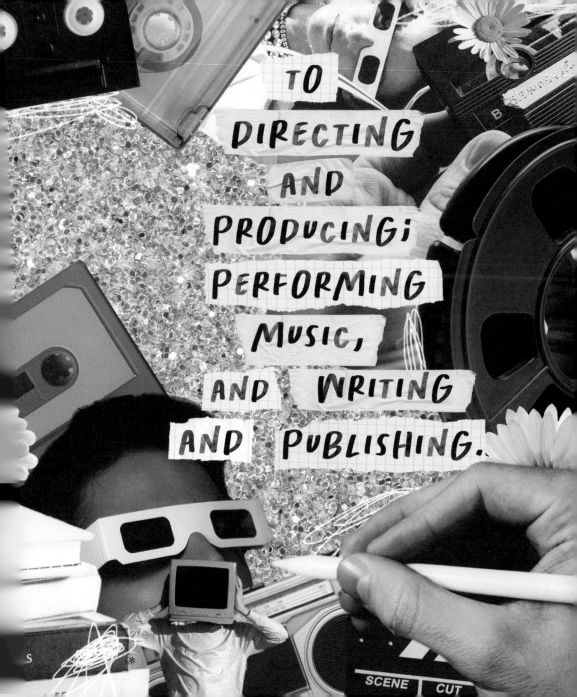

TO
DIRECTING
AND
PRODUCING;
PERFORMING
MUSIC,
AND WRITING
AND PUBLISHING.

HE'S SPAWNED COUNTLESS MEMES AND GIFS —

THE INTERNET WOULD BE A MUCH SADDER PLACE TO PLAY WITHOUT HIM.

PERHAPS IT WAS THE SAD KEANU MEME, OR *THAT* TRADEMARK GAZE,

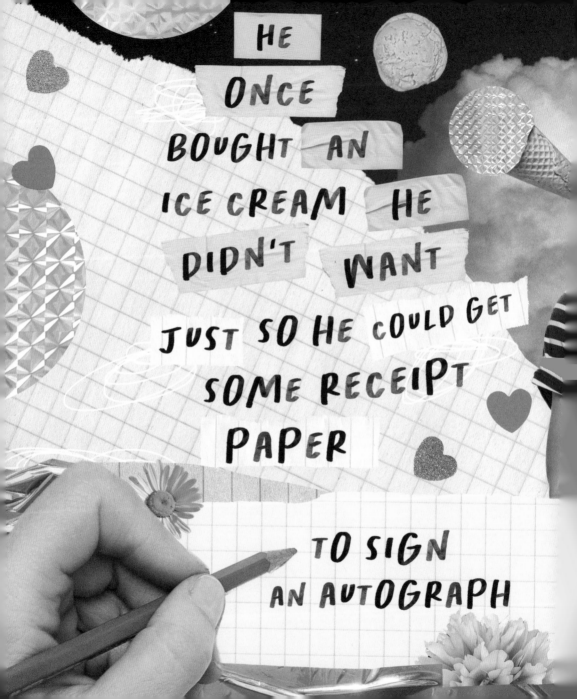

HE ONCE BOUGHT AN ICE CREAM HE DIDN'T WANT JUST SO HE COULD GET SOME RECEIPT PAPER TO SIGN AN AUTOGRAPH

FOR AN
ADORING
YOUNG FAN.

HE'S REPEATEDLY BEEN FILMED GIVING UP HIS SEAT WHEN THE CARRIAGE IS CROWDED.

NOT AVERAGE AT ALL.

IN 2019, AFTER HIS PLANE HAD TO MAKE AN EMERGENCY LANDING IN BAKERSFIELD, KEANU STEPPED UP TO HELP ORGANISE TRANSPORT AND KEPT A VAN OF FELLOW STRANDED PASSENGERS ENTERTAINED BY DJING THE ROADTRIP AND SHARING LOCAL FACTS.

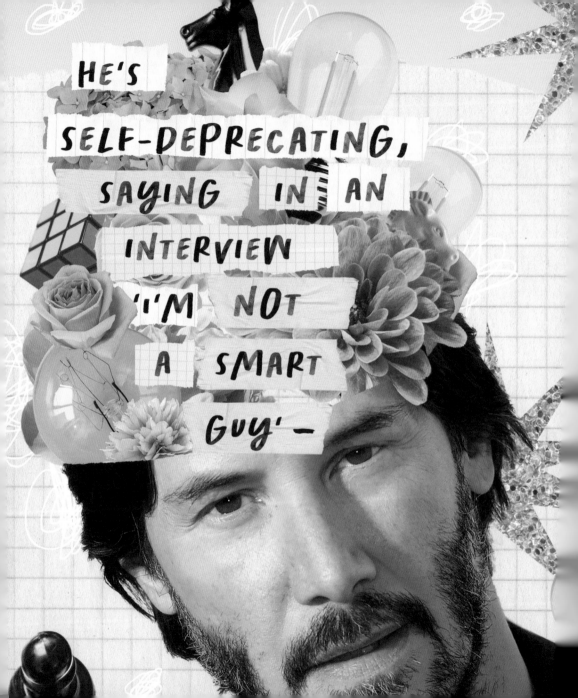

HE'S SELF-DEPRECATING, SAYING IN AN INTERVIEW 'I'M NOT A SMART GUY' –

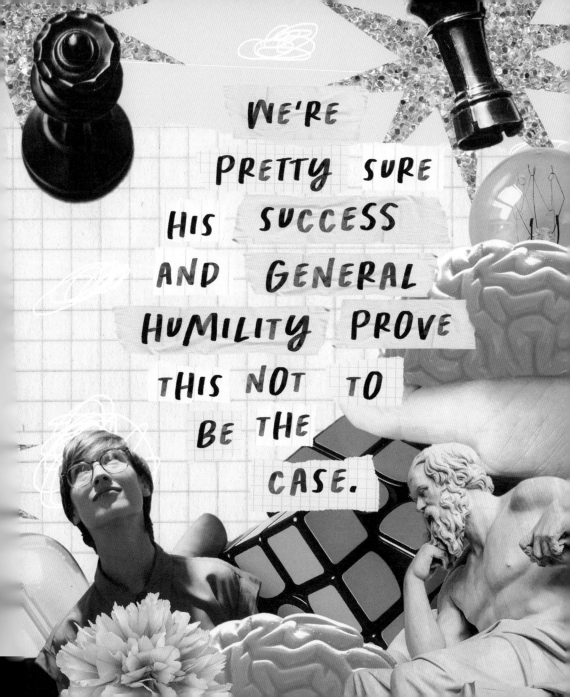

WE'RE PRETTY SURE HIS SUCCESS AND GENERAL HUMILITY PROVE THIS NOT TO BE THE CASE.

KEANU UNDERSTANDS LIFE IS TOO SHORT TO WATCH BAD MOVIES.

THERE ARE MULTIPLE REPORTS OF HIM WALKING OUT OF CINEMAS HALF-WAY THROUGH DUDS.

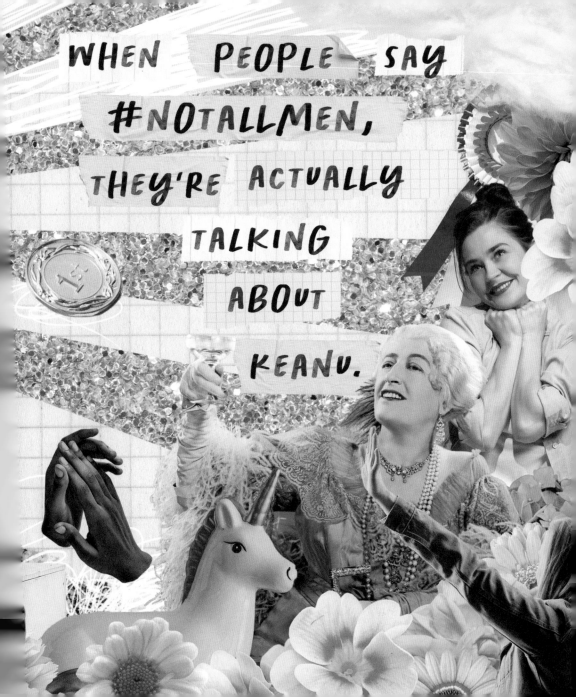

HE'S FAMOUS FOR NOT PLACING HIS HANDS ON WOMEN

KEANU IS SPIRITUAL —

'I BELIEVE IN GOD, FAITH, INNER FAITH, THE SELF, PASSION AND THINGS'.

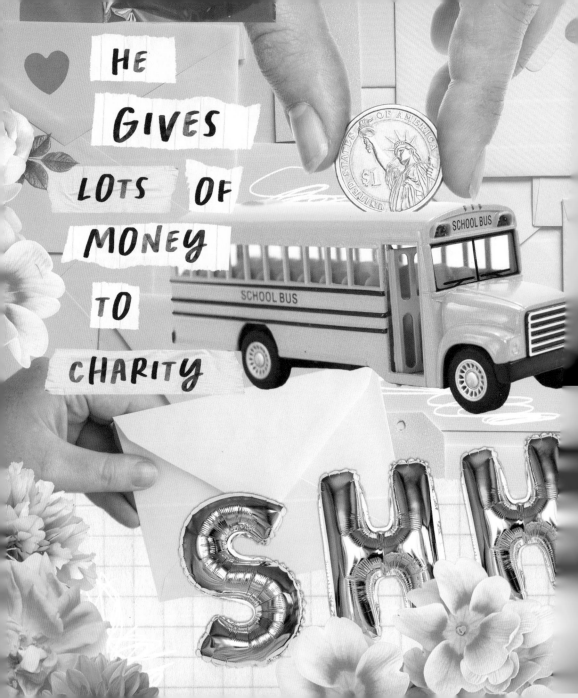

HE'S THE ULTIMATE MOTORCYCLE ENTHUSIAST AND NOW MANUFACTURES HIS OWN BIKES.

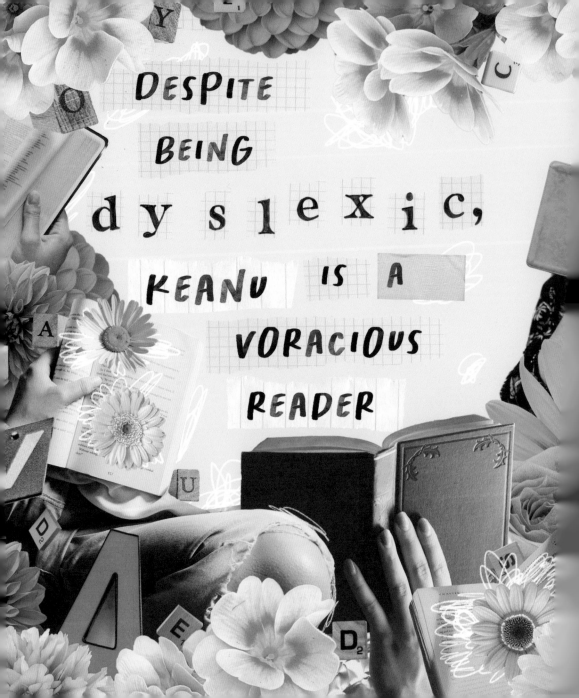

DESPITE BEING dyslexic, KEANU IS A VORACIOUS READER

AND HAS WRITTEN SEVERAL BOOKS.

HE BECAME HIS SISTER'S CARETAKER

WHEN SHE WAS DIAGNOSED WITH LEUKAEMIA

HE'S FUNNY. WHEN ASKED WHAT HIS SECRET FOR ALWAYS STAYING DOWN TO EARTH WAS?

'GRAVITY.'

HE
LOVES
PUPPIES.

KEANU'S MOVIES HAVE MADE MORE THAN $4.5 BILLION. BUT HE THINKS IT'S CRASS TO TALK ABOUT SUCH THINGS.

MORE IMPORTANTLY? HIS MOVIES HAVE 'ENTERTAINED PEOPLE.'

Smith Street Books

Published in 2021 by Smith Street Books
Naarm | Melbourne | Australia
smithstreetbooks.com

ISBN: 978-1-92581-182-7

Publisher: Paul McNally
Editor: Jen Whyte
Design and layout: Stephanie Spartels

Printed & bound in China by C&C Offset Printing Co., Ltd.

Book 162
10 9 8 7 6 5 4 3 2 1

Please note: This title is not affiliated with or endorsed in any way by Keanu Reeves. We are just big fans. Please don't sue us.

ADMIT ONE 834435

ADMIT ONE 834434

ADMIT ONE 834436

834436

ADMIT ONE 834437

834434